First published 2008
This edition © Wooden Books Ltd 2022

Published by Wooden Books Ltd.
Glastonbury, Somerset

British Library Cataloguing in Publication Data
Forest, D.
Nature Spirits

A CIP catalogue record for this book
may be obtained from the British Library

ISBN-10: 1-904263-82-8
ISBN-13: 978-1-904263-82-1

Designed and typeset in Glastonbury, UK.

Printed in China on 100% FSC
approved sustainable papers by FSC
RR Donnelley Asia Printing Solutions Ltd.

WOODEN
BOOKS

NATURE SPIRITS

WYRD LORE AND WILD FEY MAGIC

Danu Forest

with illustrations by Dan Goodfellow

This book is dedicated to the Earth Goddess and Her Lover
may they bless us all, and help us remember their ways once again.

Many thanks to John M, all our friends
and to the spirits for all their support.

CONTENTS

Introduction	1
The Web of Wyrd	2
Sacred Exchange	4
Devas	6
Powers of Place	8
Faeries	10
Families and familiars	12
Guardians and Guides	14
Spirit Doors.	16
Copper and Cold Iron	18
Seer Sight	20
Earth Spirits	22
Earth Healing	24
Earth Magic	26
Faery Flowers and Magical Woods	28
Tree Spirits	30
Sylphs – Air Spirits	32
The Four Winds	34
Raising and Calming the Winds	36
Birds and Bird Spirits	38
Wild Fire	40
Kind Fire	42
Divine Fire	44
Water Spirits	46
Befriending the Nymphs	48
Mananan mac Lir	50
The God of the Greenwood	52
The Great Goddess	54
A Magical Miscellany	56

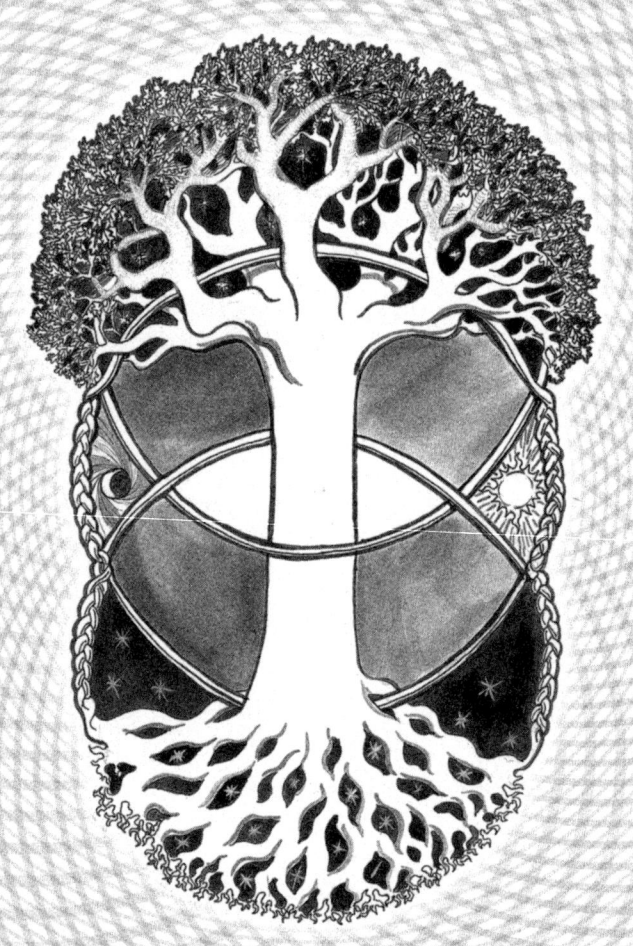

INTRODUCTION

IN THE WILD WELSH HILLS, and the craggy cliff-tops of the highlands, the splendour of nature cries out for all to hear. In such places it is easy to sense the spirits of stone, river and tree. Explorers of the otherworld know that the shadowed ravines and panoramic heights are populated with beings so different to humans that they can be terrifying, yet also so near and familiar to the stirrings of our souls that they can be almost touchable, a hairsbreadth away from our mortal fingertips, unseen and yet more real than the modern world.

Cultures across the earth testify to the existence of spirits, and every spiritual path has its collection of accompanying supernatural intelligences. Angels, ghosts, daemons and devas all affect our lives both subtly and dramatically. Traditionally, distinctions between otherworldly beings are often blurred, as they are in a continuous flow of evolution to and from the very source of existence itself. This is illustrated by the symbol of the World Tree, divided in the Celtic system into three realms: *Annwn*, the world below (the living roots), *Abred*, the physical world (the trunk) and *Gwynfed* (the 'white life'), the heavens in the branches.

Everything is nature. Nature spirits remind us, their distant cousins, of a time when we were close and understood our connection to the natural world, not merely tourists holding ourselves apart, sewing shut our eyes and ears with our endless need to consume and own the Earth from which we are birthed. In the wild the truth of this is tangible, but it also remains true in factory, flat and office block - nature and spirit are one, and we are one with them, inseparable and whole, forever.

THE WEB OF WYRD
weaving the worlds

The spiritual calling amongst humans is almost universal, as is the belief that everyone has access to a wellspring of spiritual energies. Traditionally, spiritual awareness often comes in a sudden flash, suffusing the world with meaning and beauty. Buddhists describe this as enlightenment; sensing the infinite connection of all things, a transcendence from the mundane ego-centred consciousness into something far larger. This was called 'the Web of Wyrd', by the Anglo-Saxons, *wyrd* meaning the force which binds all exisitence. They believed, like the ancient Norse, that the universe is constantly woven by three powerful goddesses, a maiden, mother and crone. Collectively called the Norns, and similar to the three Fates of the Greeks, they demonstrate that everything is connected, and all existence is one.

Just as some people seek this experience more than others, so do certain spirits, and this has a profound effect upon them. Their innate connection to Source causes powerful ripples of positive loving energy to emmanate into the world. This in turn increases their development and evolution, as well as transforming ours (and anything else they contact). Such evolved consciousnesses can become gods and goddesses. Yet, like everything else, they remain both part of the whole, and Source itself.

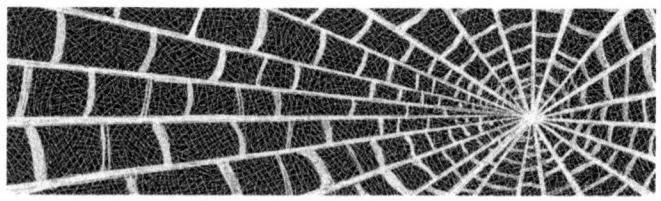

SACRED EXCHANGE
offerings, spells and prayers

As in most other countries, offerings have long been made to nature spirits, faeries and the local gods all across the British Isles, a tradition which has survived through the Christian era to the present day. In the Celtic or Gaelic traditions offerings include butter, milk, cakes and sweet things, and sometimes ribbons or small parcels of pretty cloth which are hung on tree branches. These are called 'clooties' in the West Country and can contain fragrant herbs, a silver coin, or a small prayer or petition for the god's assistance. The Celtic goddess Covetina is traditionally given silver coins in the wishing wells that were originally her special domain and consecrated in her honour.

Offerings to beings of different elements include prayer flags for air (as in Buddhism), flowers and floating candles upon water, burning incense for fire spirits, and gifts of water for plant spirits. Caring for the land in a practical way is always important and appreciated by nature spirits. Some sacred landscapes traditionally receive offerings specific to their local goddesses or guardians. The fire goddess Pele of the Kilauea volcano in Hawaii is given rum to avoid her wrath. The Yoruba tribe in Africa cast rafts of flowers upon the waves as gifts to the ocean goddess Yemaya.

In these simple ways, offerings have long forged relations and maintained bonds between mortals and the spirit realm, to call in blessings and protection in a world larger than human perceptions.

DEVAS
spirits of growth

Since food was first gathered from the forests, and later when the first crops were sown, the spirits of plants have been thanked and befriended by individuals keen to learn to tell foods from poisons, and discover the powers of magical and medicinal herbs, and the secrets of sowing and reaping—ensuring the survival of the tribe from one year to the next. Knowledge of these spirits of flowers, and all green things, spans the centuries and the continents. They are traditionally seen as glowing beings of any size which move in and out of one another and the plants which they attend.

In Hindu tradition these glowing nature spirits are called Devas. In the last century, the theosophist Geoffrey Hodson [1886–1983] and the visionary Rudolph Steiner [1861–1925] described in more detail how these beings are the spirits of plants, and their caretakers, sending them life force, and inducing their growth and fruition. More recently, the Findhorn Foundation and others have perfected techniques of working with them to produce gardens and crops of particular fecundity and abundance. Devas are traditionally friends of shamans and druids, working with them to produce greater effectiveness in their herbal medicines or assisting in potions of their energetic patterns, known today as 'vibrational essences'.

Devas hold the vision of whatever they are attached to, in its most perfect form, a belief first described by Plato [427–348 BC]. Thus a bluebell deva holds the 'idea' of a bluebell, which first emanated from the Source before it manifested in physical reality. As hive beings living in close connection with the goddess of nature herself, devas tend fields and gardens, forests and plains with equal care, enriching the green world with the breath of spirit, and infusing Earth's bounty with animation and life force.

POWERS OF PLACE
local guardians, gods and goddesses

Mankind has always seen divinity in nature, and some landscapes hold sacred status, home to powerful spirits of place. Tradition relates that in our ancestors' eyes, hills were the breasts and hips of the goddess, while gullies and ravines granted access to her depths. Mountain heights and sacred oak groves were the domain of hunter gods like Herne and Cernunnos. Dark dense forests were the realms of fierce spirits of the wild, requiring respect and even fear. Devas and elementals, local gods, faeries, animal spirits and ancestors have all coloured the landscape and been the recipients of offerings since pagan times across the globe. Our relationship with them is sometimes carved into stone and sacred objects, even painted upon cave walls.

Forests, rivers, and mountain ranges all have their local divinities, such as Tamara, the goddess of the river Tamar, and Sul, the goddess of the hot springs at Bath. The goddess Nemetona, of the druidic sacred grove, was once so powerful that she became the goddess of all sacred sites, her name becoming the public name which protected the hidden or sacred name of local gods which were known only to initiates. Barrow mounds in Wales, known as 'Cerridwens courts', come under the crone goddess's protection in a similar way, revealing the initiatory role of such structures.

The ancestral human spirits, faerie and otherworld beings resident in a particular area, as well as the earth spirits of the place, whilst all retaining their individual awarenesses, also form a collective consciousness. This contributes to the formation of the special atmosphere that such sites evoke, as well as assisting the magic and connection sought by tourists and initiates alike as they visit or dwell in such ancient places.

FAERIES
the strange and shining sidhe

Faeries can evoke both fear and yearning in mortal minds. Folklore relates how they were the first race, created at the beginning of time. Dwelling primarily in a subtle realm called by the Celts the Otherworld, that is distinct from but overlays our own, they can, according to many human encounters with them, communicate with and traverse all realms as they wish. Hive beings, their telepathic abilities are so strong as to make them almost of one mind, but they are also capable of extreme wildness and individuality. Faeries can be of any size and are often much larger than humans, but in the past they gained the title of 'little people', to play down their powers to concerned clerics, according to many folklorists and academics.

Faeries sometimes become allied with other life forms and evolve again, integrating this new energetic pattern. A popular modern belief is that they assume an appearance drawn from our minds to communicate meaning and expression, but it is not always so. Thus faeries connected to earth spirits may wear robes of crystal, or leaves. Others assume half animal forms, beasts and birds. Some have plumes of energy radiating from their heads as they attune to the deep primal energy of the planet, en route to merging with the Source. Their ways are often strange and unfathomable, and being touched by faerie can be both a gift and a curse, leaving a mortal dead, mad or a poet, as the bards relate.

The 'gentry' or 'shining ones' such as the Irish Tuatha de Danaan are so powerful as to be considered gods, and often appear to seers as very tall and beautiful with shining luminescent bodies. They are much closer to Source than humans and can choose to evolve over their vast life spans into what A.E.Russell described as 'opalescent' beings, which tend to the well-being of the planet herself.

FAMILIES AND FAMILIARS
ancestors and animal spirits

According to many traditions across the world, the spirits of ancestors and the totem animals of tribes walk alongside their people bestowing blessings and protection upon them. Befriended by prayers, dances and offerings, these spirit alliances formed the roots of the earliest societies, their images painted on cave walls and sacred objects. Everyday life was thus blended with the realms of spirit, the present with the past, and security was assured for the future, as their ranks grew with each successive generation.

A common shamanic belief is that the ancestors congregate in an otherworld hall or cave, sometimes a tipee or yurt, depending on regional variations. Across the world, the 31st of October is traditionally a time sacred to them, known as the 'Day of the Dead' in South America, the Celtic festival of Samhain and, of course, Halloween.

Witches familiars, and the 'power animals' of the Native Americans perform a similar role, teaching and supporting the survival of the tribe in relation to their environment. Hence the buffalo is sacred to the Lakota Sioux, and the tiger is sacred in Tibet. In Britain the stag signified kingship, as a personification of the hunter god. Perhaps the most sacred animal spirit in Celtic Britain was the white mare, personifying the goddess of the land, hence its image being carved so often upon the green English hills.

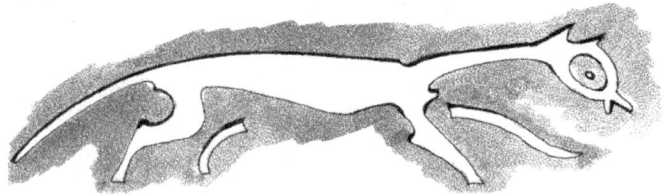

GUARDIANS AND GUIDES
cousins and co-walkers

Every nation and spiritual tradition has its guardians and guides—ancient, invisible allies that have accompanied humankind's footsteps from the cave's mouth to the present. Where Christians have angels, and Native American shamans their power animals (the spirit of eagle and bear to lend them protection and vision), in Britain Robert Kirk revealed in the 17th century how our Gaelic ancestors also had their cousins and co-walkers. These otherworldly relatives, whose lives mirrored theirs, offered help and companionship, whispering wisdom in their ears and carrying healing energy from the goddess within the land to be spread out across the Earth, via the hands of the 'cunning men', folk healers and witches.

These benevolent beings are thought to be always available to assist humans. Although their appearance can be a matter of cultural and religious resonance, a common thread is that they too benefit from giving their care. Humans, in turn, can then assist them, by their unique physicality and also by participation in the great to-and-fro of energy, in and out of manifested existence and back to the Source again.

Seers and spirit workers may have the same group of guides their whole lives, and some beings are attached to a specific bloodline or tribe through generations. Prayers, offerings and attention are always factors in gaining allies, yet the methods of connection with these beings vary as much as the cultures that embrace them, and are as unique as any other friendship.

Above: Humans have long valued their guardians and guides, unseen friends that walk through the mortal realm at their side, and whose breath on the wind brings comfort and promise.

SPIRIT DOORS
shamanic journeying

Spiritwalkers both ancient and modern use the symbol of the tree to aid their journeying to realms beyond the mortal world. Often known as the world tree, its branches reach to all times and places, its heights extend to the upper realms (the heavens and the cosmos, as well as the future), its trunk allows access to other parts of the middle or mortal realm, and its roots can be followed into the underworld, into the past and the realms of the ancestors as well as into the deep heart of the Earth goddess.

To the druids, the oak is the most powerful and significant of the trees, and its name *dara*, or *duir* in Gaelic and the druidic ogham alphabet, means 'door'. The spirit of the oak, the oak king, is considered an embodiment of the god of fertility and the supreme protector of the people, on spiritual as well as physical levels. Visualising an oak tree to assist in a shamanic journey calls upon the oak king's assistance and protection.

There are various techniques used to travel the other worlds. In some traditions the invocation of spirit allies and guardians is assisted by repetitive drumming, and the visualisation of a door which leads and grants access to the spirits or places sought. Assistance, instruction and healing is gained from this connection with the spirits, which can become an increasingly defined and fruitful experience over time. The return journey is always made by retracing the route, and grounding back into the mundane realm, often by eating and drinking.

Travelling the realms of spirit is beautiful, perilous, illuminating and confusing, and the shaman's allies are essential. To walk spirit paths is to learn the secrets of the gods, and once begun, the journey is long and rambling, growing endlessly in wonder and awe.

COPPER AND COLD IRON
cutting and mending the threads

The web of life, stretching across the universe in lines of spirit paths, rivers, ley lines and other currents of energy that form and bind all things, is known worldwide, and has been illustrated in many forms. This is the tie that binds all people and places, the flow of *chi*, the spirit cord that holds the soul to the body, the connection between loved ones and generations, binding nations and beliefs with equal ease. It is the great world serpent Ourobaros who eats its tail, and the many ancient snake goddesses.

The current of this vital life force may be dowsed with hazel forks or copper rods. Non-ferrous metals, such as copper, bronze and silver, are particularly attuned to this energy, which can be thought of as similar to lightning and water in its vibration. Conversely, iron and lead both block the flow of earth energies, sealing in life force and absorbing it. As the antithesis of the magical metals, iron is particularly known throughout faery lore to banish spirits and cause pain to otherworldly beings, hence the old use of horseshoes for protection against them.

Faeries particularly love silver, and magic was woven by the druids of the past by ringing silver bells, a sound traditionally associated with the otherworld. This draws in good spirits and builds energy, its positive vibrations ringing across the web in an endless chime of blessings and otherworldly bliss—silvery ripples across the fabric of life itself.

SEER SIGHT
cultivating devic vision

In Celtic folk tales, the many beings with one eye, one leg and one arm hint at the druidic technique of viewing and walking in this world and the otherworld simultaneously. The seers of the Celtic tradition attest to a perception of the spirits of nature and faery overlaying the landscape around them, glimmering at the corner of the eye, and being seen at will through various practices which enhance the devic vision.

As recorded by the Robert Kirk [1644-1692], author of *The Secret Commonwealth*, and folklorists such as Walter Evans Wentz [1878-1965], Celtic seers would call in their spirit cousins, sometimes sharing their eyes with trusted spirit allies, the otherworldly hosts appearing in a sudden rush all about them. This is still practised today. Increasing perception, it aids the understanding between life forms and creates a magical alliance between beings which is far greater than their individual potential.

Sometimes visions of great clarity and power may be experienced, as the devas, tree spirits and seers allies communicate meaning through symbolism and create energetic patterns which activate evolution in the psyche. Although the skill is often inherited, with patience and practice otherworldly vision can become second nature, expanding perceptions until the individual's sense of reality blends seamlessly with spirit, infusing the mundane world with magic and meaning.

Above: Second sight. This technique is best used at a place which allows views across a whole landscape. Firstly, allies are called. Then, letting the eyes relax their focus, and perhaps covering one eye with the hand, shimmering shapes and colours, shifting forms and impressions of movement may be seen. These images are particularly noticeable in tree branches.

EARTH SPIRITS
stillness, stones and crystals

There are some places across the planet where the power of earth spirits can be felt clearly and tangibly. Rocky outcrops, shadowed gorges, sacred hills, stone circles, caves and caverns sometimes hold a special energy, quiet and brooding. Heavy with the gravity of time, the stillness of rock and soil, the spirits of these places speak (to those who can hear) of the wisdom of the ever-giving Earth. Sometimes invoking fear and dread by their dense energy, these beings are known in Europe as gnomes, or dark elves, but there are many others, with many names, some now forgotten. Earth spirits and elementals consist mostly of earth energy, but can involve other elements, as in the spirits of volcanoes, where earth and fire spirits combine, or soil beings, where earth and plant spirits merge.

Earth spirits are often concerned with plants and trees, evolving into and from tree spirits, or tending the beginnings of life, deep below the surface of the soil. As crystal spirits, they hold the knowledge and memories of the Earth since its birth. The seams of precious metals and glimmering gems are the slow moving blood of the planet, endlessly pulsing with life force. Assisting the shamans and magicians of antiquity, as well as the healers of the new age, they adorn sacred artefacts from the tools of ancient Egypt, to the quartz-covered barrows of the British Isles.

Earth spirits are more easily felt in places of natural beauty where the strength and health of the earth energy is flourishing. In places where the earth is ruined their sadness and grief is painful. They are revealed in the shifts of the earthquake, and the weeds that break their way through the concrete. No damage we do is stronger than their love of earth, and they will remain strong when we are but a memory, and dust in the soil.

EARTH HEALING
the gifts of nature

Humans have long held the Earth to be the mother from which all life springs and to which all life returns. Hailed as Isis in Egypt, Gaea in Greece, and Mawu in Africa, her ancient names are endless. While humans have become like greedy children, the earth spirits work tirelessly to serve and heal her. They tend not only to places of beauty and unspoilt wilderness— the filthiest of factories and concrete-covered cities receive their care with equal love and devotion. Here they can work tirelessly, caring for and cleansing the Earth beneath, and the polluted air above.

Earth spirits will also heal people. Holed stones, sometimes called 'hag' stones, are still used in the Celtic tradition by witches and folk healers. Smaller holed stones may be used for healing by either using the stone spirit's receptive energies to draw off illnesses, or using its giving qualities to imbue the person with healing earth energy. Sometimes earth and water spirits combine to assist a healer—water poured upon such a stone is empowered and charged, and can be used to bathe the inflicted part. Crystal healing is, of course, another form of working with earth spirits.

Mankind can help the Earth in return. Asking the earth spirits to help in the garden, with open spaces, tree planting or rubbish collecting empowers these acts. A popular modern technique is to join with the earth spirits in meditation, visualising the Earth, and with them sending it loving attention and energy, which the earth spirits will direct and put to good use. Yet another way is to use a stone as a focus for the work, sending out its spirit energy, drawn from Source. Microcosm and macrocosm magically resonate to hugely amplify the energy and spread it across the whole world, even from the simplest of prayers.

EARTH MAGIC
the secrets of roots and green shoots

Sitting or standing in silence and stillness, the consciousness of the Earth can be felt beneath the feet like rising tree sap, its slow rhythms encouraging peace, and teaching the cycles of growth and decay. Strengthening and enriching, earth energies are the life force of the whole planet.

In the Celtic lands, earth spirits often have had long, if troublesome, friendships with humans. Folklore tells of how piskies and leprechauns guard places beneath the earth, and the hidden treasures of ancient kings. They are given offerings of food and drink at the entrances to their realm to encourage their friendship. In Buddhist lore, the yakshas, once the tutelary gods of forests and villages, became over time the caretakers of tree roots and hidden buried treasure. Meanwhile, Scottish trows, living in the hills of the Orkneys, are often avoided because of their love of 'borrowing'. But they mean no harm, and their love of dancing is legendary.

The ability to ground and draw off energies that have had their time is a core quality of earth spirits. They teach stability and endurance, and reveal Earth's great abundance. Their magic can be called upon when planting wish-lists under fruit trees, and their healing and empowerment can be received simply by walking barefoot upon the soil. Earth spirits are constant companions to humanity, who by their steady influence flourish like the crops in the fields and the flowers along the path.

Above: As humans have become increasingly separated from their environment Earth spirits have sometimes seemed threatening and alien to closed mortal minds. In fact, they are usually quite friendly when time is given to understanding them.

FAERIE FLOWERS
and magical woods

The growing gifts of the green Earth may be used to either befriend or repel the faeries and other spirits. When properly asked, the plant and tree allies of mortals will gather their forces to aid in human concerns. The druids burnt rowan for protection and prophetic vision (the berries are still widely carried today as protection charms). Sprigs and twigs of alder, the shield tree, have long protected travellers in this world and the next, and, when placed over the door, protect against intruders of all kinds.

Hawthorn, the goddess tree, aids in all matters of love. Its berries traditionally heal broken hearts, and its flowers bestow beauty. Elder is the home of the elder mother, who leads to Faery those who sleep beneath her branches; it is taboo to ever cut her wood. Hazel bestows wisdom, divine inspiration and grants the powers of poetry and prophecy.

Tales tell that broom is sacred to the faery queens. Sweeping with a branch of broom clears negative influences. It was also used to create the Welsh flower-maiden Blodeuwedd, as was meadowsweet, the flower of brides, also used for purification, blessing, and fertility rites. Vervain, the heal-all, anoints sacred tools and aids in scrying. Most sacrosanct of all, mistletoe, when growing upon the apple, and especially upon the oak, was the seed of the sky god and the primary power plant of the Celts.

The Oak is king of the woods, and lord of summer. His name in the druid ogham is Duir. He is the protector of the tribe and grants access to other worlds under his guidance and care. His winter counterpart is the Holly.

The Hawthorn is sacred to the maiden goddess who wears a crown of hawthorn at Beltane (often 1st May) when she weds the young hunter god. She rules over challenges and the heart. Her name in the ogham is Huath.

The Rowan, or mountain ash, with its red berries, is a tree of vision and protection, burnt by the druids to make wild fire, raising the life force of warriors and calling in protective powers. Her name in the ogham is Luis.

The Elder is a faery tree, the home of the Elder mother, a wise ancient faery who grants access to the otherworld and heals those with weary souls. She must always be treated with great reverance. Her name in the ogham is Ruis.

TREE SPIRITS
communion with the dryads

Tree spirits, sometimes called by their classical name 'dryads', are ancient and venerable beings. Beneath their many green boughs a simple air of sacredness and stillness can be found. The green and gold light shining through the leaves soothes the soul, and their quiet steady strength lends courage to the weary. Even the deva of a small sapling, via the hive consciousness of all trees of which it is a tiny part, can be very wise and powerful. Although they can assume many different forms, dryads are often human-like in appearance, albeit sometimes much taller. Venerated by the druids, who derive their name from *duir* (oak, king of the woods), trees are perhaps the most powerful spirits on the physical realm. When gathered together they form the sacred groves of antiquity, hallowed cathedrals of nature, where all living things may find their home.

These beings are usually communed with in a very simple way. Whilst sitting at the base of a tree, breathing and feeling its presence, the attention is drawn down into the trees roots, anchored and supported by the Earth. As the energy fields gradually merge, a journey in inner vision is made to meet the spirit of the tree. Good practice includes initially asking the tree how it and the surrounding environment can be helped and protected, as well as asking to be shown how to improve communication with it.

Another powerful technique, if the dryad allows it, involves breathing in as the dryad breathes out and vice-versa, forming a mutual energetic exchange. This can provide healing and insights, subtly increasing connection to the web. By such simple activities, peace and balance can be restored across the world, just as naturally as the branches touch the sky and the deep roots embrace the soil.

31

AIR SPIRITS
sylphs and storms.

Air spirits, or 'sylphs', can be felt and seen in the breath that stirs wheat fields, in the winds that shape endless vistas of clouds, and in the ripples that skim across still pools. They animate washing lines and rattle doors.

In many magical traditions they are attributed to the east, the season of spring, and their energies related to those of communication, intellect, sudden inspiration, youthful exuberance and illumination. Sylphs are especially responsive when called, and their presence is easily felt as an inexplicable breeze on a still day, or when working indoors.

They are usually friendly, even playful, and feeling their presence can be extremely pleasurable, but on occasion they can also be very fierce indeed. Weather fronts are combination hives of air, water and, sometimes, fire spirits, which form into massive beings, called 'titans' if on a planetary scale. When they are part of the spirit collective of a storm, sylphs can become very dangerous and totally unconcerned with human safety. However, like the famous Ariel, in Shakespeare's *The Tempest*, spirits of the air can also be excellent, if wayward, allies whose presence can make tired human spirits soar and the most fettered imagination reach new heights and wider horizons. Their whisper in mortal ears provokes longing and yearning, ripping away constraints and conventions with the ease of dead leaves blown across a lawn.

THE FOUR WINDS
cardinal kings of the air

Classically, there are four cardinal winds, mighty air spirits which are the equivalent of kings, known as the *Anemoi* in ancient Greece.

The first, the North Wind, *Boreas*, brings winter and night. Presiding over banishings, he freezes and blows away negative energy. Boreas aids in contacting spirits of the dead, which travel to the realms of the living on his freezing breath. He also presides over rest and deep sleep, helping animals with their hibernation, and soothing the passage into death for those with hypothermia. He brings ice, snow, and gales.

The second, *Eurius*, the East Wind, brings the spring and the dawn. He governs growth, fertility, ideas and new beginnings, youth and beauty. Eurius helps with magic and magical training, and cares for children. He brings dew and rain, tending to the first shoots, the snowdrops and the primroses, as well as the first shoots of ideas, potential, and all living things. He is 'inception', the 'first breath' upon the waters, at the very beginning of creation.

Thirdly, the South Wind, *Notus*, brings the summer and noon. He presides over matters of love, passion, and fidelity, as well as prosperity, maturity and longevity. Notus brings the energy of life in full bloom, of parenthood and comfortable responsibility. He brings warm winds, and is especially helpful in easing drought.

Finally, *Zephyrus*, the West Wind, brings autumn and evening. He presides over testing and initiations, spells and matters of healing and release. Closely connected to the moon, he oversees dreams, intuition, and deeper magicks, sometimes known as 'the Mysteries'. He brings clarity from confusion, but also shields with mist and rain.

CALLING THE WINDS
binding the breeze

Few sounds are more evocative than the howling of the wind on a dark night. Wind spirits are traditionally harbingers of the Irish *beansidhe*, the Cornish spriggans and the Slavic veelas, the storm women with their terrible fearsome beauty. Veela sometimes appear as swans, and swan feathers are used to hold power over them. Raising and calming the winds was a vital skill for shamans and mariners of the past, as the breath of the spirit world was carried on the earthly winds and could bring either blessings or disaster.

Scottish witches called the winds by banging stones in wet cloth upon sacred boulders. Ancient Finnish seafarers ritually bound winds into three or more knots tied in a rope to the ship's mast—this is similar to the Greek technique of binding winds in a cloth bag, only for them to be let loose a little at a time when needed. Of course, great offerings were made to compensate and pacify the air spirits for their confinement.

Air spirits can be called using wind instruments, e.g., a penny whistle. They are respectfully asked either to calm down or raise up, before the sylphs are sung or played to, and visualised dancing and moving to the music. It is the rhythm and feeling of the music that is important—its expressiveness and intention. It can be nonsensical, simple and repetitive, 'la-la-la', for example. Then the rhythm is gradually changed, slowing bit by bit soothingly to calm the winds, or speeding up with increasing passion to raise them. Dancing with the wind with rhythmic and expansive movements can be also powerful. The more they are communed with, the more the sylphs will be sensed, invigorating and inspiring all who contact them, infusing a windy day with magic and wonder.

BIRDS AND BIRD SPIRITS
magical feathers and flocks

Birds and their great spirits have long been the allies of humans, as they arc across the sky and hover on the winds. Poised and precise, the eyes of the hawk and the spirit of the eagle are the helpers of shamans across the world, teaching spirit flight to the upper realms. Celtic bards wore swan feather cloaks, called the *tugen*, as objects of power for this purpose, swan spirits being guardians of poetry.

The Celtic ogham script was said to be inspired from the shapes of the crane on land and in flight, and the crane was also sacred to bards. The secret tools of both the shaman and the storyteller were hidden within a craneskin bag, as cranes guided the journey to the underworld.

Shamans today still journey to meet bird spirits, collect feathers and study their flight and songs. The raven and the crow both reveal the touch of the crone goddess, her magic visible in the shimmering colors in the black of the ravens wing. The eyes of the owl are also the eyes of the goddess who sees between the worlds and into the heart of every being, seen and unseen.

The flights of these and other birds across the sky traditionally formed an augury where their movements reflected ripples on the web of life, portending events to come and reminding those far below of places unseen, distant horizons and the wonders of the air.

Above: Bird spirits can be seen in the weaving twisting swarms of starlings arcing across the Somerset wetlands in autumn. Anyone who has seen a flock of birds in flight must attest to their collective consciousness as they move across the sky as one.

WILD FIRE
fire spirits, serpents and salamanders

Fire holds a special place in the human imagination. Its flickering light danced upon the cave walls that sheltered our ancestors in the furthest past, and the shadows it cast drew images and symbols of the spirit world, close enough to touch but impossible to grasp. The fire spirits were considered the kin of the Sun god in ages past, and offerings were burnt as gifts to them to ensure the Sun's return. Essential for warming, cooking and bringing light, they ignite the human spirit with vision and divine illumination, instilling passion and courage.

The afrits and djinn of Arabian folklore consist entirely of divine flame, and were the messengers of magician kings whose power depended totally upon their sometimes unwilling service. The legendary Pheryllt (druid fire masters and early alchemists) dedicated themselves to the study of fire, believing that the spirits of all things manifested as smoke when burnt, this forming the basis of their study of spiritual transformation.

Both fire and fire sprits have long been associated with spiritual energy. Tales of the burning bush and the history of eternal flames, tended by the Vestal Virgins and the priestesses of Brigid in Kildare are testimony to its role, representing spiritual transformation and mastery. Life force or *kundalini* is also known as the serpent fire, which allows greater access to divinity within the person as it is raised through the body.

Above: Salamanders are the basic form of fire elementals. Like dragons, they are both the flame and the fuel of the fire, and are invoked in ritual to represent the element of fire, and the direction of south.

KIND FIRE
spirits of the candle flame

The soft golden light of a flickering candle is a powerful symbol—it calms and comforts, encouraging hope and stillness. A solitary flame is all that is needed to utterly transform darkness, within or without. Often used for meditation, it both represents the soul and lights the way in order to commune with it. Candles are common features in temples and churches for the same reason, the living flame guiding the way to spirit where brighter light would forbid such subtle shifts of consciousness.

It is important to remember that candle flames are fire spirits, with as much power and potential as the greatest inferno, volcano or forest fire. Consciously connecting with these flickering sparks of divinity, and lighting a candle with special intent is powerful in its simplicity.

The spirits of candle flames are wise and transformative, despite their brief lifespan, and have been questioned and conversed with for millennia, from the time of Solomon to today's modern Wiccans. This is done by opening the perceptions, and observing and interpreting the weaving, twisting and bowing movements of the flame, which form a kind of body language. Whether beholding a candle, hearth or bonfire, gazing into flames is often hypnotic and rewarding.

Candles are also useful for spellwork, as developed by medieval magicians. Specifically coloured candles anointed with special oils or inscribed with relevant symbols are burnt with magical intent to align with the desired outcome, often by correspondence with astrological or angelic forces.

Although they must be respected, the divine spark of fire and flame burning into the darkness, and the sleeping embers of a banked hearth are a sacred gift to mankind, warming bones and hearts from the cold.

DIVINE FIRE
the lightning flash

Sudden and sharp, ripping the sky with silver daggers, the lightning flash is the most magical and majestic of fire spirits. Created without human contact, it manifests as suddenly as it vanishes. Lightning, as a spark from heaven, contains all the power and energy of Source and divinity, and in one awesome instant can change everything that it strikes forever.

The druids taught that lightning is particularly powerful when it strikes an oak tree, associated with the gods of storm such as Taranis, Thor and Zeus. Lightning-struck oak is a powerful talisman, and such trees were of primary importance to ancestral druids as the energetic fusion of earth and sky. Lightning has always been honoured and feared, as it signifies the divine inception of mother earth by father sky.

It is possible during thunder and lightning to open up one's aura and energy field to the divine chaos of the storm, and be swept clean of energies that are no longer needed, as well as receiving sudden illumination. Caution is strongly advised, but exposing bare flesh to the elements without going to a dangerously exposed spot during such extreme weather is often enough to be of benefit. The aim is to feel the air and rain which the lightning rides, rather than to be struck. With intent and invocation, the energy will penetrate the body and unblock stuck areas of illness and dis-ease on all levels.

To work with lightning requires bravery and honesty, not bravado or macho foolishness. Lightning rips away all that is past and redundant, so it is best not to hold on to illusions. Instead, meet these spirits as a vulnerable mortal, intelligent enough to respectfully ask their assistance. Try not to provoke disaster. Be illuminated rather than destroyed.

WATER SPIRITS

mysteries of shore and wave

Nymphs and mermaids, merrows, selkies and nixies—spirits of the water invoke longing and wonder. Glimmering beneath the moon, their mistress, they serve the tides, currents and the gods of the sea, Lir, Mananan and Poseidon. The relationship between humans and water spirits is deeply entwined with the tales of lonely fishermen, and sailors washed up upon foreign shores. However, water spirits are also known to befriend whole families and communities, intermarrying and raising children who belong in both worlds.

There are tales of Scottish fisherman taking selkie (seal maiden) brides by stealing their sealskins and binding them by ancient magical laws. Such marriages are said to be loving, but always end with the beautiful selkie returning to the ocean, leaving behind children gifted in sailing and storytelling, and husbands silent and alone, looking endlessly out to sea.

W. B. Yeats relates how a burial ground in Ballyheigh in Ireland was drowned by the merrow king, to reclaim the bodies of his half merrow family. He also tells how a crofter called Dogherty was great friends with a sea spirit called Coomara, who collected the souls of drowned sailors in lobster pots in his home beneath the waves, thinking he was doing them a kindness. As strange and treacherous as the sea, the spirits of water are kind and dangerous by turns according to rhythms no mortals can fathom.

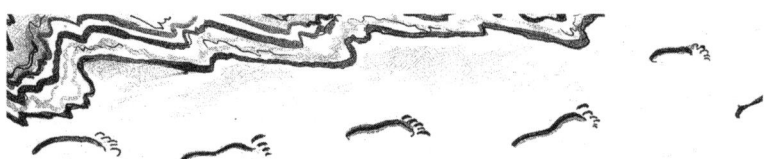

Above: Central to the magic between humans and sea spirits is the shoreline, a boundary where the realms of earth and water endlessly struggle back and forth. According to Celtic lore, the power of earth recedes entirely at the ninth wave, beyond which the rules of earthly kingdoms are relinquished to those of the watery depths.

BEFRIENDING THE NYMPHS
sacred springs and holy wells

Sacred springs and holy wells hold special significance for mankind, as the spirits of rivers and lakes run like the life-blood of the planet, supporting the health of human, plant and animal life, and encouraging settlement and agriculture. Cultures across the world have revered the spirits of water for thousands of years, worshipping the goddesses of wells, rivers and lakes for their life-giving waters, binding their people with the realms of water spirits through offerings and sacred tales. Myths abound of the Greek sea nymphs, and there are countless tales of the Lady of the Lake, the magical faery mistress of Avalon, who grants healing to the weak and weary, protects Britain's sacred treasures and guards the sleeping king Arthur.

The Celtic goddesses of holy wells, such as Covetina and Sulis, are still honoured by silver coins cast in their waters—silver representing the moon, their mistress, who reigns over all beings of water and wave. Visiting sacred waters at the full of the moon is a powerful ancient practice, as the vision of moonlight reflected upon water was used by Celtic seers for centuries for augury and access to the otherworld.

The selkies' song, drifting over the waves on the shores of the Herbrides was a call to mortals to remember the sacred pacts between the people of Earth and the people of Lir, the sea god. It is said that a single tear of a seal maiden upon the waves will cause a storm, and gifts of flowers and other offerings cast on reedy rafts upon the waves ensured plentiful fishing and safe passage across this treacherous kingdom.

Connection with these beings is made today in the same way, and over time lends a deep soulfulness to life, as the nymphs of spring, river and sea refresh and unlock access to personal longings and dreams.

MANANAN MAC LIR
charming and calming the waves

Mananan mac Lir, who gave his name to the Isle of Man, is a god of the sea and an ancient ally of the Celtic peoples, especially the honoured kings Bran and Cormac to whom he gave several magical gifts, including the famous silver branch. He often appears in myth as a noble warrior with silver hair, like his father, the sea god Lir. According to a description contained in the 7th century tale *The Voyage of Bran*, his underwater realm is an otherworldly pastoral vision, and at its heart is a crystal castle, which is the home of the selkies, the seal folk and other magical water spirits.

Mananan could be called upon to grant safe seafaring, as the Celts were great mariners. It was traditional at first to make an offering to the sea god such as a glass of mead, or some flowers. Then, it is thought that he and the accompanying spirits would be sung to, in rhymes such as "*Mananan mac Lir; Make the ocean smooth and clear; Let us sail without fear; Mananan Mac Lir ...*" with accompanying to-and-fro dancing, reflecting the motion of the waves. Mananan and others that had assisted would then be thanked. If the god had allowed it, there would be calm seas and safe passage, but if not the souls of the drowned sailors would join in the feasting in his glimmering kingdom far beneath the waves.

Above: Mananan Mac Lir is the legendary first settler on the Isle of Man, often considered the magical centre of England, Scotland, Wales and Ireland. Each year at midsummer the Manx people cast rafts of flowers upon the waves to honour him and ritually pay respect and give thanks for his continuing protection.

GOD OF THE GREENWOOD
laughter amongst the trees

Sometimes friendly, at other times terrifyingly wild, the god of nature, the Green Man, Pan or Herne is the male face of nature, the resurgent life force of the forest and the field, retreating in winter to burst forth with new exuberance in the spring.   Various tales tell of how he is cut down, whether as Osiris, John Barleycorn, the Oak King or King of the Bean, only to miraculously rise again. As such, these are all forerunners of the Messiah story, for he signifies the growth of the green world, sown and reaped by turns in the cycle of the year. As Jack in the Green, famous in folklore, he is a young god, full of tricks, laughter and great feats of prowess. He often runs along ley lines and is famed for his supernatural speed and huge leaps. Drawn by innocence and enthusiasm, he can help weary souls become children of nature once again.

In other tales he appears as the god of hunters. As Herne or Cernunnos he has simultaneous roles as god of animals and 'He who culls', ensuring the survival of the tribe through harsh winters, and can be called upon to teach maturity and responsibility. As the oak and holly king, the god of summer and winter, he is the dual father of the people, providing security and sustenance, protecting and providing the people's needs.

The Greek god Pan reveals another side of the god of nature—the god in repose. A wild rustic god of sexuality, drinking, music and fierce pleasures, his greatest friends are goats, and his fits of passion can create the 'panic' in mortals of which he is famed. Today, Pan is loved by so many that he is now often seen as an almost universal god of nature.

Though sometimes worshiped alone, the god of the greenwood is the divine male in all his aspects, lover of the goddess, father to all creation.

THE GREAT GODDESS
the many faces of mother nature

Mother goddesses have been worshipped from the time of the earliest civilisations, giving birth, as they do, to the Earth and all of nature. Gaea, Demeter and Rhea to the ancient Greeks, Ishtar in Babylon, Isis in Egypt, associated with the Earth, the Moon, Sun, and all the elements, the great goddess has many faces, the common thread being her divine feminine nature, and her fertility. She embodies all stages of womanhood, as well as all aspects of nature, plants, animals and the Earth itself. The mother goddess is equally welcoming to all, and is still worshipped today in many forms, despite her widespread overthrow by numerous patriarchal systems. She is called upon with songs and offerings, and contact with her always has profound effects, especially on women.

In England she is known as Britannia, who gave her name to Britain; and as Sil (of Silbury the Harvest Hill) she is the ever pregnant goddess of the land, a goddess of abundance and harvests, her round belly and breasts forming the curves of the land. In Wales, the ancient mother goddess was known as Modron, meaning simply 'mother', becoming Matrona to the later Celts. She was also known as Andraste, the protectress of the Iceni tribe, as invoked by Boudicca against the Romans.

In Ireland she is Danu, Eriu and Flidais, the goddess of the woodlands, who rides a chariot drawn by deer, a hunter goddess like Diana and Artemis. As Boan, the cow goddess, she grants fertility and is goddess of the river Boyne. Goddesses are often associated with water as well as earth, for water is the prerequisite of life itself. As the Earth, her body is shaped by mountains and rolling hills, so rivers and oceans are her lifeblood, and the fertile soil, her womb, endlessly births life itself.

APPENDIX - A MAGICAL MISCELLANY
tools and techniques

PROTECTION

Those that travel between the worlds never do so alone. Always call upon your guides and allies. Ideally your first journeys or rituals should be to call upon these and begin developing relationships with them. Deities of all kinds are also called upon regularly, depending on cultural and religious resonances. Some people merely call upon 'the light' or 'Source' to guide and protect them. Offerings and spirit songs are made to give thanks for the assistance, whether it be from spirits, power animals or sacred protective plants, as well as deities. Working in a magically charged circle provides a separate and sacred space which protects from unwanted or uninvited energies. Iron and salt are powerful protective talismans from otherworldly beings, as are rowan or alder twigs, especially if the trees have been asked to empower them first. There are also protective runes, ogham sigils and symbols such as the pentagram which are all very powerful, and can be drawn in the air, upon objects, or even visualised. The best protection however is awareness. Listen to your gut reactions, avoiding beings or directions which feel wrong, and instead follow and encourage that which feels wholesome. There is no need to fear, which creates its own negative patterns, but instead master any fears by awareness of the self, which will improve your experiences in all worlds.

GROUNDING

Before and after all magical workings it is essential to 'ground'—to become calm, centred and present in the everyday world. A few deep breaths from low in the chest, and taking time to feel your feet on the ground, earths and calms. When journeying or performing ritual, taking time to eat and drink afterwards re-integrates the soul back into the body and settles the energy field. This is a good time to write notes on your techniques and experiences, which can provide invaluable insights and patterns to be discovered over time, as well as making sure the connections formed or information received is properly remembered when consciousness is returned to a normal state. It is important not to overdo your spiritual work, and to take things a step at a time. However, if difficulties are experienced it is important to stay calm and parent yourself back to a balanced state. Eat, breathe, hold grounding crystals such as obsidian, or stones like granite. Place your feet on the soil. There are a number of vibrational essences available in health food or magical shops that also help. Also remember there is always protection to call upon to help you feel more secure. Work physically with the body, walk about, clean the house etc. place yourself firmly in the ordinary world. In a short while you will feel normal again, and stronger for stretching your psychic muscles.

ENERGY RAISING

Energy raising is achieved by many means. Tai chi, chanting, drumming and ritualised dance all raise life force, but several meditative techniques are also very powerful: Placing your feet on the earth, imagine the infinite earth energy in the ground below, and visualise this rising up through the feet. Similar to the Hindu tradition of activating the chakras, this energy rises up the spine and across the body, filling it with energy and light. This can then be passed as an offering up to heaven forming an energetic link. This creates subtle energetic changes in the body and aura, healing as well as energising, and restoring the flow to blocked areas. The same technique can be used to draw energy down from the sun, heavens or stars into the body and down to earth. Every time the flow and connection is made or restored anywhere in creation, there is healing, blessing and growth. The energy can also be directed with intention for magical purposes, to heal or charge up magical tools or energise spells, or be sent lovingly to a nature spirit of any kind to establish friendship or for healing. Used in partnership with others or nature spirits, it can be redirected across the Earth, to heal and rebalance the environment, or any of the elements in a given area. To help the planet as a whole, simply join the nature spirits, as if holding hands, and, visualising the whole planet, direct the energy from above to the planet as a whole from this perspective. The energy will then be directed by the nature spirits and the goddess herself to areas where it is most needed.

CLEARING, CLEANSING AND BANISHING

Allies and deities can all be called upon to clear an area of negative energies. Directing energy raised from earth or above can also clear and bless. Certain plants and crystals also help. Drawing a protective circle with iron or steel will make negative entities flee, and cutting an imagined cord of the web connecting yourself to an undesirable being is very effective if done with clear intent. Sweeping peppermint oil over the aura also disconnects any energetic parasites or latched energies. A famous Native American technique is 'smudging'. Burning sage or 'smudge sticks' works very well to clear cleanse and banish negative or stuck energies, and can be performed whilst working with earth, fire or air spirits to heal an environment of unhealthy vibrations. Simply ask and thank the spirit of the sage for its assistance in clearing the area, and sweep through the area or around an object to remove any negate entities or energies. The earth spirits will aid the sage spirit, the air spirits will further empower the smoke, and fire spirits empower the fire that burns the sage—working in unison, this simple act becomes immensely powerful. Always remember to have something to catch the ash and water to put it out if it burns too vigorously!

THE FOUR DIRECTIONS

In traditions as diverse as medieval magic, witchcraft, druidry, native American spirituality and quabalistic magic, the four directions of the compass are commonly related to the four elements. The East is linked with air, intellect, illumination, communication, dawn, youth and the gestation of ideas / projects. The South is related to fire, passion, instinct, kundalini, creativity, noon, adulthood and the development of ideas/ projects. The West relates to emotions, dreams, intuitions, sunset, maturity and the fruition of ideas and projects. The North relates to earth, stability, silence, physicality, age midnight death and the still, fallow point where new growth is the emerging seed beneath the soil. Elementals of each direction can be asked for assistance with corresponding issues, or all may be invoked for increased balance and energetic harmony, or circle work.

THE CIRCLE O

Contemplating the significance of the circle is an almost universal spiritual and magical practice. Reflecting the circle of the Earth and the seasons, as well as the spinning of the Milky Way, the circle represents so many spiritual truths as to be of primal magical importance. Circles are 'raised' by magical practitioners and shamans to create a sacred space protected by the circle's defining line which separates the space from all other dimensions and unwelcome influences. Only that which is either in the circle at its raising, or that which is invoked, is able to exist within its confines. Circles are 'drawn' by directing raised energy in a circular shape around you, and improved by invoking the four directions at the cardinal points, thus enlisting the elemental energies to further empower it.

THE WHEEL OF THE YEAR ⊕

In general pagan practice, the circular pattern of the seasons is called 'the Wheel of the Year', marked by the eight 'spokes' of the festivals which mark the main solar points and the other four moon-based festivals, both of which relate to the agricultural year. These are the two solstices at approx Dec and June 21st, and the equinoxes of approx Sept and March 21st. The other four are Beltane (May 1st) Lughnasadh (Aug 1st) Samhain (Oct 31st) and Imbolc (Feb 1st). These events are important, as marking them assists in aligning with the ebb and flow of energy along the web and thus increasing awareness and empowerment. They are also doorway points between the worlds when exchange and interchange are easier. Faeries in particular migrate at such times.

THE LUNAR WHEEL ☽○☾

The waxing and waning of the moon also has a powerful influence on nature and the web, and patterns of reaping and sowing have long been carried out in harmony with it. The moon is usually seen as a goddess, whose three faces correspond to the moon's phases of waxing, (maiden) full (mother) and waning (crone), relating to the three phases of womanhood. The full moon, time of the witches Sabbat, is a time of great power for manifestation and empowerment, assisting in attuning with nature spirits particularly plant and water beings who will be more tangible and active at this time. However, the new and dark moon is a good time for connecting with the vibrations of the earth spirits, contacting the ancestors and accessing 'the mysteries'.

OGHAM

The ancient Irish tree alphabet, usually carved off a vertical stem, was used exclusively by the druids, for the marking of graves and monuments, but also for oracles by the branch of druids known as the filid, or oracular poets, whose task was to be the memory-keepers, the guardians of ancestral and traditional lore. Ogham for them was a symbolic and magical system which used the example, image and metaphor of the trees and their energies to signify and open up whole vistas of meaning accessible only to a magically elite and learned few. Although each ogham letter corresponds to a tree, and in the 20th century was given the added correspondences of months in a tree calendar by Robert Graves, their meaning is not limited to the tree they represent, but can be unlocked over time by meditation on the tree and associated quatrains and kennings, contained in the few surviving texts that provide the sum of knowledge on the ogham, especially the 7th century 'Scholars Primer'. However, these symbols have a power of their own, and their unique spiritual energies can be invoked for simple divination or magical purposes. They are divided into five aicmi (tribes). Sometimes a further five, the 'forfeydha', are included, but they are a much later addition to accommodate consonants not included in the Irish alphabet.

A very basic and simple interpretation of the ogham is as follows:

1) Beith - Birch - Beginnings (cleansing)
2) Luis - Rowan - Protection (protective)
3) Fearn - Alder - Defence (protective)
4) Sailed - Willow - Harmony inspiration
5) Nuimn - Ash - Strength (empowering)
6) Huath - Hawthorn - Challenge and love
7) Duir - Oak - King - Fate (protective and grounding)
8) Tinne - Holly - Energy/ Chi (protective)
9) Coll - Hazel - Wisdom (inspiring)
10) Quert - Apple - Wholeness (for healing)
11) Muin - Blackberry - Harvest
12) Gort - Ivy - Support
13) Ngetal - Fern/Reed - Preservation
14) Straif - Blackthorn - Magical power
15) Ruis - Elder - Sacrifice
16) Ailm - Scots Pine - Overview/ far sight. (clearing)
17) Onn - Gorse - Fertility.
18) Uath - Heather - Earth/ goddess/ luck
19) Edadh - Aspen - Movement/ change (eases fear)
20) Idho - Yew - infinity (grounding)

THE PENTAGRAM ✪

An ancient pagan symbol, signifying the four elements of earth, air, fire and water, with the fifth, spirit. The circle around it can signify protection, and the world. Also represents the goddess. Used for protection, empowerment, charging magical items, invoking and banishing, it can additionally be used for blessing, as it represents the harmony of the goddess, the balance of the universe. Reversed it is known as an earthing pentagram, pointing down and directing the energies earthwards. It also represents the horned god. It has nothing to do with Satan, everything to do with Venus, and is helpful and positive in its effects.

THE AWEN /|\

A Celtic symbol, also known as The Three Rays. Represents the three worlds, the three paths leading to Earth, heaven and faery. The three races: human / faery / animal. The triple goddess / triple god, mother / father / child. Invokes inspiration and harmony. Used in otherworld journeys for safe passage. Shows a friendly traveller the way. Chanted to encourage vision, invoke spirit harmony and right action.

THE TRIPLE SPIRAL 🌀

A Celtic symbol of the Goddess as maiden, mother and crone. Represents the three realms. Protective and blessing.

THE SPIRAL 🌀

An even older symbol than the triple spiral, it represents the spinning of the universe, the movement of planets around the sun and the passage of time. Also the endless outpouring of creation and its reverse. Therefore symbolic of the breathing in an out of the Source itself. With nature spirits it forms a basis for common understanding, and thus like the triple spiral and the awen attracts assistance and can grant safe passage in otherworldly realms.

THE VESICA PISCIS ◖◗

The sign of two circles overlapping is a very ancient symbol of a the goddess as interdimensional portal, via her birth canal, the vulva-like shape of the circles intersection. The two circles represent the earthly world and the otherworld, among other interpretations.

DOWSING

Dowsing is a general term for various methods of divining earth energies and finding water sources, amongst other uses. Thin forked hazel branches or copper L-shaped rods are held loosely but steadily straight ahead of the practitioner, who walks slowly around a landscape, sacred site etc. Currents of earth energy, spirit roads, threads of the web can be detected by a clear and definite movement of the rods that is unintentional and distinct. Other dowsing methods include the use of pendulums which reveal yes/ no answers via back and forth or circular movements. Pendulums are particularly useful when dowsing over a map rather than whilst walking.

RATTLES, DRUMS & MAGICAL GARDENING

Simple percussive instruments have been used by shamans across the world for millennia. Repetitive beats assist in changing consciousness, shamanic flight and spirit invocation. These instruments, like other magical tools, have spirits of their own which can be honoured and befriended. They also have practical as well as spiritual applications, for example, using a seed-filled rattle when planting or sowing. Invoking earth, plant, water and fire (solar) allies creates a ritual aspect to the universe and has commonly acknowledged positive effects on the plant's growth. Some rattles are also useful when calling in rain spirits, via the similarity of the sounds created. This draws upon a magical law of like-attracting-like, known as 'sympathetic magic'. It is for this reason that drumbeats are so useful for journeying, as they resonate with the heartbeat, in turn transforming the traveller's energy field and state of consciousness.

SSSSHHH

The most important technique is the most simple. Learn to listen, learn to feel ... try not to tell the world or the spirits too often how clever you are, how powerful or how psychic, and try not to tell them endlessly how bad, lost or small you are either ... it is not really important, and adds to the endless deafening human chatter that blocks the way for so many. Instead, try to spend some time each day just listening; to the wind in the trees, to the birds singing, to the messages from your loved ones and from spirits alike. And each day, try to feel the wind on your face, the rain on your cheek, and the gentle tugging, shifts and callings of your own spirit, and your own unique thread of the web. Maybe some will notice the change in you, most will not, but in time your pulse will beat in rhythm with the heart of the Earth herself, and your spirit will shine with the brilliance of the stars.